INTENTIONAL

Practical Principles to Experience Success in Every Area of Your Life

Andrea Evans-Dixon

Copyright Notice © 2020 Andrea Evans-Dixon,

All rights reserved, including any right to reproduce this book or portion thereof in any form whatsoever.

This book is designed to provide accurate and authoritative information concerning the subject matter covered. It is sold with the understanding that there is not a professional consulting engagement. If legal or other expert advice or assistance is required, please consult with a licensed professional in your area.

Scripture quotations marked NIV are taken from the Holy Bible, New International Version of YouVersion 8.16.4. Copyright © 2006-2015 The Android Open Source Project.

For information on bulk orders or have Andrea Evans-Dixon speak at your next event, please contact Andrea at andrea@successfuldiva.com.

Disclaimer

This book is designed to bring awareness to various behaviors and habits one can incorporate into their life in pursuit of purposeful living. The author does not claim that the principles shared in the book will guarantee success. The information shared within this book highlights a few lifestyle changes that the author has incorporated to experience a higher level of mental, physical, spiritual, financial, emotional, and overall professional success. Sound efforts have been made for content accuracy. You hereby agree never to sue or hold the author liable for any claims or similarities arising from the information contained within this book. Any likenesses to real persons, alive or deceased, or personal experiences are merely coincidental. You agree to be bound by this disclaimer.

Dedication

This book is dedicated to three groups of people. First, to those who genuinely want to experience higher productivity, fulfillment, and achievement. More notably, this book is dedicated to those **willing** to take **intentional** action towards creating a more productive life. Lastly, to those who are eager to take deliberate action towards having more positive, destiny-filled experiences, personally and professionally. I stand in the belief that **YOU** are ready.

WHAT'S INSIDE

Disclaimer iii

Dedication iv

Acknowledgments vii

Foreword viii

Introduction 1

Success Principle #1 ~ Protect Your Mind 4

Success Principle #2 ~ Time Management 11

Success Principle #3 ~ Be Still 17

Success Principle #4 ~ Learn to say "NO" 22

Success Principle #5 ~ Invest in Yourself 27

Success Principle #6 ~ Take a REAL Vacation 32

Success Principle #7 ~ Your Fab 5 37

Success Principle #8 ~ There is No Competition 42

Success Principle #9 ~ Pivot Lessons 47

Success Principle #10 ~ Speak Life 55

Success Principle #11 ~ Be Great Without Apology 59

Success Principle #12 ~ Gratitude is the Great Multiplier. ... 63

About the Author 69

Acknowledgments

Living intentionally requires dedication and, in some instances, accountability. There are those whom God has placed in my life to hold me accountable, but there is only one individual who holds me accountable and is not threatened by the purposeful and deliberate way that I manage my life and, more or less, our lives.

To my husband, J. Fred Dixon Jr., although we have been married for 13 years, you have been a part of my life for many years before our marital union. From the beginning of our friendship, you welcomed my independence, encouraged my growth, and supported and nurtured my vision for the business. Most importantly, you have always prayed for and with me. You are everything that a strong, self-sufficient, black woman like me could desire in a husband. You are my angel on earth, and I thank you.

Foreword

Time is filled with swift transitions, along with many life and living adjustments. As we experience more of this episode called life, we should also be intentional about strategically making life plans to accommodate the rapid changes in life and keeping up with its demands.

Let's first understand the word intentional. According to the Oxford Dictionary, intentional is done on purpose; this suggests that you must make a decision.

Life and living as we know it is of the past, which has unapologetically moved us into another dimension of life to look at every area of our lives and make the necessary adjustments to survive and succeed.

It takes discipline to be intentional. There will be days that mediocrity would try to force itself into your life's schedule and slow drag you into a mood that will eventually cause you to become unproductive and unsuccessful. However, being intentional is the power needed to thrust and thrive in life. Life needs a plan with intentional steps of executions that will provide you the power to live a successful life. Let's be clear about that word success. Success is not all about money and material things. The first sign of success is having and maintaining the attitude that you are eligible for success. Success is not a secret. Success is discovered, embraced, and engaging. You must become intentional about your accomplishments of life and self-convincing of your destiny. Your life is not in the hands of any human individual but in the hands of our creator God, who is the giver and sustainer of life. They can only co-sign your signature. God has already given you what you need to be successful. You have to come in an agreement with Him and accept His plan for your life. Faith without works is dead. No work, no success. Success does not happen because you said it, dreamed it, or wrote it. Success happened because you WORKED IT! You can't complain about the results you got because of the work you didn't do.

There are many steps and factors in achieving the successes you want. The first step is to ask yourself why you want success. If there is no why there will be no "when." Success has to be placed in a category with strategic and intentional plans. Each day that you live, it should be lived on purpose. It's meaningless to awake every day with no sense of direction of that day or in life. It is often said that the early bird gets the worm. I tend to believe it's the hungry bird that gets the worm. You have to be hungry and then feast on the proper thoughts and actions that will fulfill your hunger that will forward you those opportunities that will cause you to thrive in life and living.

In Colossians 3:2, the words "set your affection on things above" means to place your mind and thoughts on them, show favor towards them, and be affectionately desirous of them. Be very careful about what you give your mind, mouth, and thoughts to. What you say will determine the directions your life that will take you to or from. When you become of age, accountability, and responsibility, you can no longer use your childhood excuses as an escape from being a productive adult. Take charge of your thoughts, words, and actions to become and have all that God has designed for you in life and living. SUCCESS is yours if you want it.

Intentional,

Dr. Kevin B. Parrott

Introduction

Life comes complete with seasons. It is full of ups, downs, highs, lows, achievements, failures, laughter, tears, and I could go on and on. I believe you understand my point. Yet, there comes a time when a person begins to ascertain what is essential in life. We ask questions like, "am I living my best life?" "Is this truly important?" "What legacy do I want to leave for my children?" "Is what I am doing getting me closer to fulfilling my dreams?" "What do I consider success to look like?" If we are honest and diligently seeking to live first, in God's will, and second on purpose, all of these questions and more are valid and should be pondered not just once in life, but occasionally over one's entire life.

I have (finally) discovered that intentional and purpose-filled living is essential to experience God's best. No matter where you are in life, and no matter your age, God has plans for you to prosper in every area of your life. Be encouraged. It's okay to persist and be relentless when striving to be your best. Notice that I did not say strive to DO your best. I said to strive to BE your best. Who are you being? Most of us have grown up believing that we had to do more than someone else to be successful. Well, I am here to share without apology that doing does not always guarantee success. In your doing, who are you being, or at a minimum who are you becoming? God knew all about you and I BEFORE we arrived. He created each of us fearfully, wonderfully, and unique. There is only one me and there is only one you. We can be imitated but never duplicated.

Approximately five years ago, I began to affirm over my life the mantra "Success is Intentional." As this affirmation took root, I began to focus on my life areas that I could either improve or change. It is a necessity to conduct periodic assessments of your life – personally and professionally. An assessment allows one to evaluate and measure growth or the lack thereof. The 13 Success Principles documented in this book have been invaluable to the way I approach my day. These success principles help me maintain balance, avoid burnout, keep first things first, remain encouraged, dispel doubt, and on and on. In short, placing these principles into practice allows me to do everything I can to **E**levate **(my life) Intentionally Towards Excellence and Success.** The keyword being intentionally. My company, **ELITES Beyond Measure Inc.**, was born out of the lifestyle I set forth to live and the desire to help others to do the same.

As you read Intentional, I challenge you to conduct a full and honest assessment of how you live. I dare you to implement one, two, or all of the success principles you will read in this book. Let me warn you. Change does not and will not happen overnight. If you are not already accustomed to thinking positively, intentional success-driven thoughts will require patience. You will need to rewrite some falsehoods that you may have learned in childhood. Inevitably, to make a change, there must first be a mind-shift. You must begin to view yourself as successful long before it may be evident to the world.

Everything achieved is created twice. First, in your mind and second in reality. Consider this. Could the reason you are not

Introduction

living the lifestyle you desire, earning the income you deserve, or even starting the business you have dreamed of owning be as simple as not having a clear picture of it in your mind? Could it REALLY be that simple? I believe that you are reading the right book at the right time. I desire to provide you with some of the success principles that have helped me live better, enjoy each day even when things don't go as planned and elevate my thoughts into alignment with what God says about me. It's not too late to begin to speak over and into your life those things that you want to see. If you are currently not living your best life, intentionally, I urge you to start today. In addition to reading this book, connect with someone you view as living an intentional life. Give yourself the time to make the necessary adjustments. Whatever you do – do not give up. The world is waiting for you to show up…..INTENTIONALLY!

ELITES
Elevating Lifestyles Intentionally Towards Excellence & Success

Success Principle #1 ~ Protect Your Mind

Philippians 4:8

"Finally, brothers and sisters, whatever is true, whatever is noble, whatever is right, whatever is pure, whatever is lovely, whatever is admirable – if anything is excellent or praiseworthy –

THINK about such things."

New International Version

Success is the result of deliberate thought, followed by action. There is no hit or miss. Merriam-Webster's definition of intentional is "done by intention or design." It lists a few synonyms of intentional, such as conscious, deliberate, purposeful, and willful. Each of these words is the opposite of accidental. Those who experience the success that lasts over time are not better than you or I. They simply "think" differently.

This success principle begins with Philippians 4:8 because this is the fundamental essence of protecting your mind. To gain control and be a protector of your mind, start by thinking about what you are thinking. You may be saying, "Diva Andrea, how do I think about what I am thinking? I can't help it. Sometimes thoughts appear in my mind without notice." Well, some thoughts do randomly show up, but you have the power and control to dismiss any thought that is negative or goes against your desired good. You hold the key. By your thoughts, you can transform yourself. Your thoughts radiate outward in the form of words. Those words attract both good and evil in your life. Biblically speaking, this is the essence of sowing and reaping. Your mind is a conduit – a channel – through with your life, subsequently places these thoughts on display. A negative mind **cannot** produce a positive life.

    I am an avid reader. One of my favorite authors is Wayne Dyer. He transitioned from life in 2015. I am grateful to have been introduced to his books and teaching early in my entrepreneurial career. Although I did not apply the principles right away, I discovered enough to know that he was a devoted advocate in helping others create the lifestyles they deserved to live. Once I became serious about living a different lifestyle and intentionally building success, I referred back to some of the principles introduced to me through Wayne Dyer's book, "Wishes Fulfilled – Mastering the Art of Manifesting." I encourage you to read Wayne's book for yourself. However, I will summarize the five action items that I have incorporated into my daily routine with the specific intention of protecting my mind.

1) I use my imagination.

Let's think back to when we were younger. Okay, go a bit further back to when we were children. Our imaginations were unlimited. We were unstoppable in our minds. Anything was (and still is) possible in our imagination. My imagination allows me to focus on the good that I desire to see manifested in my life. I use my imagination to visualize the best pictures of my life, health, businesses, family, or anything I desire. Be patient! If you have not used your imagination for quite some time, this requires work. It takes time to let go of doubt and forget about who, when, and how. Using imagination allows us to live today as if our desires have already become a reality. Wayne states that "imagination is the greatest gift." Anything that is to be created or proved must first be imagined. In essence, your mind must arrive at your destination before your life does.

2) I strive daily to live each day from the end.

This concept, for some, may seem hard or even impossible. Yes, even for me, this principle took a lot of practice. I must intentionally center my mind on the result, the goal, and the most important steps I need to take to propel myself forward rather than look at what is going on with others or the world. One of my examples of living from the end is within my Mary Kay business. I attended my first major conference as a consultant in 2005. Seminar is a conference that is held annually in Dallas, Texas. At this event, I saw women going across the stage for various achievements. The women were in gala style, floor-length gowns. Their hair was perfect, and their smiles were larger than life itself. When I returned from that Seminar, I committed to returning next year, having earned a diamond bumblebee, which would grant me the opportunity to grace the stage with my elegant style, floor-length gown, perfect hair, and larger than life smile. Before I knew what power this principle had, I can look back and say I was living from the end. As I worked my business throughout that next year to earn my place on stage, I practiced my walk, my wave, my smile, and even the handshake that I would give to the National Sales Director on-stage who would present me with my award. I lived from the end. So, I ask. What are you thinking? What do you desire to see as a reality in your life? Take time to live in your mind from the successful completion or achievement of your desire.

3) I assume the feeling from the end.

This one is directly associated with living from the end. Feeling it means precisely that – FEEL IT! Feel the success in your soul. Allow your face to show how excited you will be once you have achieved your desire(s). How will it feel paying off your car? How does the aroma smell in your bakery or restaurant? How will you feel as you are signing the closing documents of your first home purchase? The feeling is what you feel in your body as you visualize your desired result. When you learn how to live in the feeling and what you want is in alignment with God's will, you become it, and it becomes you.

4) I give attention to what I desire.

Being intentional requires attention. I have discovered that when I place my attention on something, it's a done deal. No matter how long it takes, if I focus on it, it will happen. I had to learn how not to allow my attention to be sidetracked by the external pressures when they arrive. One of the phrases that I state to others (and myself) is this, "There is never a time in life when all the lights on the streets of life are green at the same time." Red and yellow lights of life, which I will call "external pressures" are real. They sometimes light up unexpectedly. You must be extremely intentional about what you decide to give or not give your attention.

It is here where the power that we possess to control our thoughts requires the most intentional practice. Why? What you give notice to is what your subconscious mind takes ownership of. I have had the honor of leading and coaching many women. As their leader and business coach, I am responsible for listening to their goals, the amount of money they desire to earn from their business, and assisting them with a plan to reach their desired outcome.

Along with this task, more often than not comes a time when I must guide them around or over the hurdles of external pressures. What are the external pressures? These are the situations, things, or people that (could) become distractions. Distractions are sometimes in disguise, and at other times they are quite visible. It takes a determined and made up mind to not allow a distraction to override your desire for greater. I encourage you to only give attention to what you want to see more of in your life.

5) My thoughts are positive before entering sleep.

I did not grow up in the household with my parents reading bedtime stories to me. However, whenever I watch a child going to sleep as a parent is reading or telling a story on television, I envision a child's mind and what is being processed. Their consciousness allows them to slip into that state of rest. Wayne Dyer declares that the last five minutes before entering sleep are vital to ensure that your desires are fulfilled. I have proven this to be true. Each day of my life has been immensely impacted by what I am doing before drifting to sleep. For example, if you go to bed angry, you will more than likely wake up angry. The thoughts that are hovering around in your mind right before sleep have a direct impact on your next day. Today, my most common daily actions before going to sleep are writing in my journal, reading, prayer, and meditation. It is rare for me to go to bed while watching television or a movie. If I am closing my day with a movie, I intentionally meditate for five minutes and say a prayer just before going to sleep. The critical point you want to grab from this opportunity to protect your mind is that as you transition into sleep, you want pictures of positive, beautiful, successful, and the like. How you prepare for sleep is more important than sleep itself. Read that sentence again if you'd like. When I journal before going to sleep, I ALWAYS end my journal entry with things that I am grateful for from that day. My closing thoughts in my journal are those things that I intentionally thank God for in my life. Even if the day has not been a good one, I choose to close my day and henceforth channel the thoughts in my mind upon that which I am grateful. There is ALWAYS something to be grateful for, and since my subconscious mind (and yours) never goes to sleep, I want to download and program into it the things that I want to experience more of each day.

Protect Your Mind Prayer

Dear God, show me your way. Whether I need to make new friends or break old habits, I want to align my thoughts with how you see me, act pleasingly, and live in your will. Amen.

Success Challenge #1

Take 5 minutes twice per day, morning and night, to visualize good coming into your life. Envision the achievement of your next desired accomplishment. If it helps, write it down.

ELITES
Elevating Lifestyles Intentionally Towards Excellence & Success

Success Principle #2 ~ Time Management

Ecclesiastes 3:1

"There is a time for everything, and a season for every activity under the heavens."

New International Version

What is time management, and why is it so crucial to your success? As a child, teenager, and even young adult time management was probably not a significant factor in your day to day routine. Neither was it for me. However, as an adult and in particular, as an entrepreneur, time management is essential. If I am honest, I am a master at time management, and I hope that what you are about to read will give insight on how you can be masterfully effective in this area.

Plainly stated, time management is the systematic prioritization of tasks. Each task is typically assigned a start and end time. In business, time is money. Poor time management can not only cost you money but also prevent you from performing the necessary tasks to grow your business. Even if you are not a business owner, effective time management is key to maintaining balance with work, the schedules of your children, and any other activity that you want to complete within any given period. Additionally, effective time management will cause you to be more organized and lead to less stress.

Think about the ways that you may have wasted or not optimally managed your time? Facebook? Talking on the phone? Checking email? Or how many times have you ended your day with tasks that were not completed? The good news is you can improve your time management skills. It is this success principle that ensures that I successfully navigate each day with intention.

Plan your work and work your plan. You may be saying, "Diva Andrea, I plan my work, but working the plan is another story. A good plan to manage your time MUST be in writing. We live in a digital age, and I know that it has become more common to keep everything within the cell phone's data walls. However, there is something powerful and biblical about writing it out and making it plain. I use my cell phone to record my appointments, but I still use the good old-fashioned, paper, wire-bound calendar that I call "my datebook." Regardless of my phone, I do not confirm anything until I have had a chance to verify my availability from my paper datebook. My datebook displays every task scheduled on any given day between 6 am and 9 pm. What? Yes! EVERY TASK that I intend to complete appears in my datebook. Thus, it is fair to say that it does not get done if it does not appear in my datebook. Meditation, prayer, exercise, conference calls, any medical appointment for myself, my husband, and parents, breakfast, lunch, dinner, office time, date night, client appointments, events, social events, church-related events, etc. Do you get the point? My datebook is a detailed, itemized, time-allocated visual of my day, week, and month.

So, what happens when something emerges that was not planned in my day? Here's an example of something simple that sometimes does appear, but was not initially planned in my day. One of my customers could call me with a request to purchase a Mary Kay product. They are heading out of town and need to receive delivery of the product today. From my datebook, I can quickly determine if and when I can provide service to that customer. I can advise precisely when, in my day, it is best to fulfill the request. I am not stressed. I don't have to manipulate my time or interfere with anything else on my calendar. Remember, effective time management begins with a plan – preferably written.

    Now, what if something emerges that is not as simple as the example used above. One day my husband's truck would not start as he was preparing to leave for work. He discovered his battery was dead. Naturally, this was not in my datebook. However, I had to decide on how to best assist him in getting to work. There are times when situations arise that are not as important as ensuring that your spouse gets to work. As an entrepreneur, I have developed a method that has allowed me to assess situations not initially in my datebook to determine if I should allocate time within my day to it. **Remember, some situations that arise are distractions in disguise.** Distractions, if not handled properly, are time management wreckers. Should you find it challenging to keep your attention on what is necessary to move your day forward as planned, what you are about to read could be your solution. When something arises that was not initially planned in my day, I take that situation through what I call the "Triple D Process." The Triple D Process is my way to ascertain what role I need to play, if any, to what extent the particular situation warrants my attention, and how the situation impacts my day.

DEAL WITH IT (in other words DO IT) – Does this situation REALLY require my attention now, or can I take care of it later? Believe it or not, everything that someone asks you to do or brings to your attention does not require immediate attention. With a little thought, you may discover that you can delay your involvement and give the matter some attention when it does not interfere with your productivity. If the issue requires my attention, then I will deal with it. Choosing to deal with a matter requires that I think quickly on how my involvement impacts the day. Please understand that if you do not have your day written out and well planned, you will not know what must be rescheduled or you will become frustrated because you feel pressured to do it all. As you improve your time management skills, you will find that when you must deal with a matter, you have the unique capability to shift appointments or previously scheduled commitments with ease.

DELEGATE IT – Here's a news flash……some situations do not require your **direct** involvement. Delegating permits others and empowers them to handle a circumstance. Delegate as a verb means to entrust a task or responsibility to another person. Your act of delegation could be conditional and necessary only for the situation at hand, or it could be something that you permanently hand over to someone else. Who knows? Your ability to delegate could be the one thing you need to establish better time management skills. Thus, do not get overwhelmed or frustrated by unexpected incidents or requests from others. On the contrary, think of who else could handle it for you.

DELETE IT (in other words DON'T DO IT) – When a situation arises, or I am presented with a task that seeks my

Success Principle #2 ~ Time Management

attention, and I decide NOT to do it or in other words, I opt to say "no," I have made the immediate decision that the situation is not critical enough or it is not a priority. I have learned to say no without apology. Since I have dedicated an entire success principle to the power of the word "no," I will say that if something is truly not worthy of your involvement, don't do it!

Time Management Prayer

Dear God, I am so blessed. Your daily provision is sufficient, and the hours of each day are enough to accomplish everything I need. Forgive me for the time that I have wasted. Forgive me for complaining to you that I do not have enough time. Grant me the wisdom to use my time each day to bring glory and honor to you in everything I do. Amen.

Success Challenge #2

On Sunday evening, take the time to plan your week. Review each day and write out precisely what is to be done every hour of your day. We live in an electronic era where calendars are on our phones. However, for this challenge, I recommend a datebook that you can manually write-in your daily activities.

ELITES
Elevating Lifestyles Intentionally Towards Excellence & Success

Success Principle #3 ~ Be Still

Roman 12:2

"Do not conform to the pattern of this world, but be transformed by the renewing of your mind. Then you will be able to test and approve what God's will is – his good, pleasing, and perfect will."
New International Version

You hold the key to your thoughts. What you radiate outward from your thoughts in the form of words you attract into your life. Biblically speaking, you reap what you sow. The mind in which thoughts cultivate is a conduit between our inner being and who shows up. Yes, you can sometimes fake it. However, the curtains will come down on that act.

So, how do you begin the process of taking control of your thoughts? This process requires renewal. How does renewal occur? Stillness. Silence. Calmness. Tranquility. Quietness. Relaxation. All of the words you have just read require you and me to BE STILL!

Before leaving the corporate arena in 2005, I recall having time off in the form of what was known as "personal days." What did I typically do on a personal day off? Probably what most people do on a personal day off; I ran errands, made visits to my doctor or dentist, and did everything BUT REST! I had to learn how to physically, emotionally, and mentally rest. Why is rest a learned behavior? Because as adults, we no longer get the luxury of taking the scheduled nap as we did in nursery school or pre-kindergarten. We, especially those of you who are parents, have greater responsibilities than we did before the age of 18. We have replaced rest with the hustle and mentality of climbing our way up the corporate ladder. Now, I am not saying that we should not aim for the top or obtain the education and necessary skills that will better our positions to earn income. Nonetheless, what I have learned and come to appreciate dramatically is that long-lasting, tangible, sustained success cannot be obtained without God's blessing. Practicing rest is a spiritual discipline that helps me enjoy God's presence and realign with his plan for my life.

One of my favorite books of the Bible and chapter is Psalm 23. The entire chapter is God's promise of provision. Verses 2 and 3 of this Psalm states, "He makes me lie down in green pastures, he leads me beside quiet waters, he refreshes my soul. He guides me along the right paths for his name's sake." New International Version. When I finally took an inventory of what these two verses mean, I realized that God requires rest. Rest allows me to remove myself from the noise of the world. It is difficult to hear God speak when our daily environments often contain so much noise and chaos. Whether you are an entrepreneur or not, I encourage you to make time to be still.

Busyness makes us feel like we are accomplishing something. Yet, without healthy boundaries, your busyness may be only routine and numbing you to your need for intimacy with God. When was the last time you indeed took a personal day for yourself? When something is personal, it is all about you. Today, as an entrepreneur, I take at least one personal day per month. Yes, that is 12 personal days. That's more personal days that I was ever granted while in corporate America. Additionally, my husband and I take at least two REAL vacations per year. I will share later in this book what I qualify as a REAL vacation. I don't know about you, but I never received 12 personal days while working in the corporate arena. For clarity, a personal day is not the same for me as a vacation day. What I do when I take a personal day may vary. Here are a few examples of how I spend my personal days:

1) Go to the movie theater and watch two different movies;

2) Spend the day at a spa;

3) Sleep in and spend the day at home reading, meditating, and communicating through prayer with God;

4) Take a drive to another city to have lunch and do some shopping;

5) Take an extended personal day and stay overnight at a hotel for a private retreat.

Each of the activities listed above permits me to "be still" and withdraw from my daily routine. A personal day should be a sabbatical from your daily routine. Now you might be saying, "Diva Andrea, I have children, and doing the above or anything similar to it is impossible." My response to you is that it is only impossible until you do it. You may not be able to take a full day, but I encourage you to start with a few hours and decide what you can do to refresh yourself within those few hours. I am confident that you will discover that two, three, or even one hour in stillness can be very rejuvenating.

The important thing is that you take time to be still, refresh, and renew. Making a personal day for me means that I do not answer the phone unless in the case of an emergency. My husband and anyone close to me knows how to reach me should there be an emergency. For some of you, simply not answering your phone or responding to Facebook could be a personal day. I'm just saying.

Thus, before you dismiss the importance of a personal day and what relaxation or being still can do for you, allow me to share some of the benefits. When you and I take the time to be still:

1) It can lead to a happier viewpoint when maneuvering through the demands of daily living.

2) It has proven to create more lasting, positive memories because the brain waves are more relaxed.

3) It builds a more robust immune system. Being still allows the immune system to operate a full capacity.

4) It helps to improve relationships. Stress negatively impacts your relationships more than you can ever comprehend. Stress out couples quarrel, fight, and withdraw more from each other. When you have taken time to be still and relax, you are more able to give and receive love.

5) It leads to better sleep and increased energy.

6) It promotes greater and enhanced creativity.

7) It can reduce some of the pain experienced in the body. Being still allows me to turn inward and let my mind

communicate with areas of pain. Those who meditate often refer to this as mindfulness meditation.

8) It may lead to expanded motivation and inspiration.

Be Still Prayer

Heavenly Father, you have promised me abundant life, and I want to enjoy all that you have divinely planned for me. Help me slow down and take the time necessary to renew my mind and body when worn. You know my daily responsibilities. Yet my daily duties are not higher than you. Show me how I can spend more time in your presence. Teach me Oh Lord how to BE STILL! Amen.

Success Challenge #3

Schedule a personal day on your datebook. Share the date with your partner, husband, and children if applicable. Remember, it's okay if your personal day is only comprised of a few hours. Be sure to indicate a method of how family members can reach you in the event of an emergency.

ELITES
Elevating Lifestyles Intentionally Towards Excellence & Success

Success Principle #4 ~ Learn to say "NO"

James 4:7

"Submit yourselves, then, to God. Resist the devil, and he will flee from you."

New International Version

This success principle can be intimidating yet rewarding. Unpopular, yet necessary. No one enjoys being told "no" and telling someone "no" can be frightening. However, learning the art of saying "no" can be one of the best productivity tools you have ever used.

If you have read my book, Pitfalls of Entrepreneurship, you will recall that I dedicated an entire chapter, also known as a pit, to share what can happen when you refuse to learn the art of saying "no." I feel the need to revisit this area in this book because learning how and when to say "no" is a success principle that separates you and me from the crowd. Success is never convenient. Anything worth having is worth working for and making a temporary sacrifice. We are who we are by the choices we make. God gave us a mind to think with and the opportunity and freedom to choose. Using the word "no" is a choice. Being intentional requires that we understand when to say "no" and, on occasion, accept "no" from others.

Success Principle #4 ~ Learn to say "NO"

When we have a dream, vision, or calling, I believe this is God's way of giving us a peek into his will. Here is a little secret. Your dream, your vision, or your calling, is precisely that – **YOURS!** Have you ever heard the statement "what God has for me, it is for me?" Of course. In pursuit of experiencing what God has for you, I contend that you will undoubtedly have to say "no" to someone, something, or maybe even go through a season of not having things go quite your way.

Many people want success in various areas of their lives; however, they are unwilling to change the things necessary or do things differently to experience success. Success is never by chance. Success is never convenient. However, real, sustainable success is undoubtedly intentional. What about luck? Luck is success or failure brought *by chance* rather than through one's actions. When we do as God asks us to do, which is to commit to the Lord whatever we do, He will establish our plans. It's a promise. He plans to prosper you and me, and our God is always intentional.

Take a look at this picture. What or who do you see?

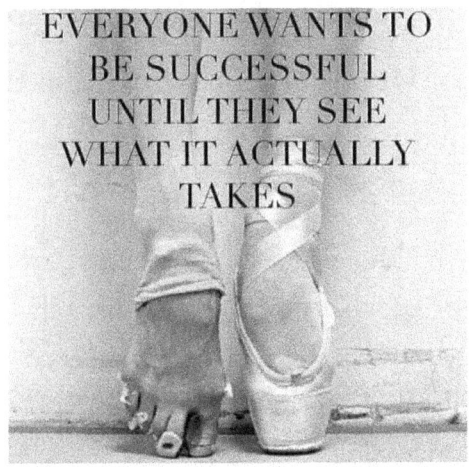

Intentional

Here's the obvious: The feet of a ballerina, one foot with a shoe, one foot without a shoe, band-aids, and bloody toes. However, allow me to challenge your imagination of what is not so apparent by presenting the following questions:

1) How long has this person been a ballerina?
2) How many hours per day does this person practice?
3) What has this person given up for success?
4) How many people told this person they would never be successful?
5) What sacrifices have been made?
6) Why is this person putting themselves through this obvious pain?
7) Has this person reached their intended success or not?
8) How many birthday parties, social outings, or other events has this person declined to attend?
9) How many tears have been shed?
10) What dream has been placed in this person's heart?

As you ponder the above questions, what resonates with you as possible answers? To what extent does your ability to say or not say "no" impact what it takes for you to succeed in starting your business, expanding your business, becoming a better ballplayer, or simply learning a new skill?

Success Principle #4 ~ Learn to say "NO"

When it comes to your success, learning to say "no" requires discipline. Since we are not privy to everything that God has designed for our lives, we must trust Him. Whether we are saying "yes or no" to things or people, we must do our best to be in God's will. God always finds a way to steer me into the direction I should have taken if and (most likely) when I make an incorrect decision. Others may not fully understand, like, or even agree with my decision to decline their request. Guess what? You will have those who do not understand you either. The good news is what God has for you is for you, and someone else's understanding is irrelevant.

Learn to say "NO" Prayer

Father in Heaven, you have given me a mind of my own and the freedom to choose! I want to make choices that align with your will for my life. Give me the courage and strength to say "no" when I should. Help me not to take it personally when someone tells me "no."
I desire to stay focused on and in your will.
Amen.

Success Challenge #4

1) *Make a list of at least five situations when you have been told "no." Reflect upon each case.*

2) *Make a list of at least five situations when you should have said "no." Reflect upon each case.*

3) *Make a list of at least five situations when you did say "no." Reflect upon each case.*

   How do you feel as you think about each situation?

ELITES
Elevating Lifestyles Intentionally Towards Excellence & Success

Success Principle #5 ~ Invest in Yourself

Luke 5:36-38

"He told them this parable; No one tears a piece out of a new garment to patch an old one. Otherwise, they will have torn the new garment, and the patch from the new will not match the old. And no one pours new wine into old wineskins. Otherwise, the new wine will burst the skins; the wine will run out and the wineskins will be ruined. No, new wine must be poured into new wineskins."

New International Version

Personal growth has a profound impact on every area of your life. Before I go too far into this success principle, allow me to state, although money can be used as an investment into yourself, your investment does not always require money. In fact, each success principle in this book can be considered an investment in yourself. To invest means to devote, empower, give time to, give power, or place effort.

If you have lived long enough, worked on anyone's job long enough, raised a child/children, made an attempt to become an entrepreneur, or you are currently an entrepreneur, there has come a time when you have had to learn a new skill. New skills may be acquired in the form of education, experience, or merely changing the circle of people with whom you associate. In other words, there must be an intentional commitment to growth.

The scripture quoted at the beginning of this success principle references a parable that Jesus spoke to the disciples. A parable is simply a story used to illustrate a lesson. Jesus used them often in the Gospels. I believe that if we do not take the time to invest in ourselves, it is the equivalent of trying to place new wine in old wineskins. Consider the following:

1) Parenting your 18-year-old in the same manner as you did when they were your 4-year-old. "No, new wine must be poured into new wineskins." ~ Verse 38 You must grow and develop new parental skills for your 18-year-old versus what was used to parent your 4-year-old.

2) Playing a sport at the collegiate level with the same skills you used when playing at the little league level. "No, new wine must be poured into new wineskins." ~ Verse 38 You must invest practice time to develop the advanced skills required to compete on a level with others who have advanced skills.

3) Operating your business with the skills today that you began your business with 2, 5, or 10 years ago. "No, new wine must be poured into new wineskins." Verse 38 Today's technology and the World Wide Web have demanded that we obtain new skills or hire persons who have those skills to operate successfully.

Success Principle #5 ~ Invest in Yourself

The new wineskin is you, and your growth represents new wine. Growth cannot stand on commitment alone. Growth requires a plan, time, and precise identification of the area(s) you desire to see your progress. Here are a few examples of how I have invested in myself:

1) Reading. I am not against fictional writing, but as I began to seek and follow God's plan for my life and the desire for my businesses to grow, I find myself more intrigued with books that elevate my thinking and belief in myself. Refer back to Success Principle #1.

2) Networking. This investment allows me to share, learn from others, and exhibit my products and services. After all, if I have a service or product that meets the need of someone else and vice versa, we have both been a blessing to each other. Networking has led me to other people whom I did not know previously. These people are commonly known as referrals. When done properly, networking can provide a considerable return on your investment.

3) Workshops/Conferences. When I attend conferences or seminars, I go with an expectation of God delivering something that I need to hear. I attend events with the **intention** that I will leave with what was meant for me to receive. Besides, who wants to waste time or money? I don't, and nor should you.

4) Success Principle #3. If necessary, return to this principle and reread it.

5) Hire a Personal/Business Coach. Coaches can keep you accountable for growing yourself and your business. Additionally, they can help you remain focused. Even coaches have coaches. I am a living witness. I encourage you to consider bringing a professional coach on board for your personal and business growth rather than merely having friends with opinions. We will dive more into friends in Success Principle #7.

I encourage you to be one of those persons who will be aggressive and obtain whatever training is necessary to be all that you can be in life. Choosing to do nothing and complaining because no one is dropping opportunities into your lap is pointless. Be willing to invest in yourself. Henceforth, making yourself more valuable to your employer and one day as an entrepreneur.

Some of the above methods require a monetary investment. However, these are only suggestions and not an all-inclusive list of what you can do to invest in yourself. Additionally, you do not have to execute all of these things at the same time. As it takes time for a financial investment to show results, the same is true when you decide to invest in yourself. Time is a necessity. When you choose to invest in yourself, it means that you have also decided to embrace and welcome change. Although all change is not good, some change is necessary to develop. When you are purposeful about the changes you want to see and the timeframe in which you'd like to see the change, investing in yourself becomes more natural, and you will learn to view it as an asset to your growth rather than a liability. Learning is a lifetime process. I believe that we can all learn something every day. The more you know about what you are doing, the more confidence you will have. The more confidence you possess, the more confidence others will place in you. Life and its evolution position each of us in God's classroom to be a lifetime learner.

Invest in Yourself Prayer

Lord, your word tells me that the hairs on my head are numbered. Your investment in me, the giving of your son's life on the cross, cannot be measured. I don't want to be left behind in my life because of my laziness or unwillingness to invest in myself. I want to experience everything you have divinely orchestrated for me, and I know that requires growth! What are you trying to teach me today? I welcome the lessons that you will send my way. Amen.

Success Challenge #5

*Take a personal and business assessment. Have you reached a goal initially set this year? What investment did you make in yourself to achieve that goal? If your evaluation is not favorable, commit today, and choose an appropriate action as well as a financial investment if necessary that emphasizes you. If your action step requires finances that you currently do not own, begin saving **today** towards that action step. In the meantime, select a more immediate action step that does not require as much from your finances.*

ELITES
Elevating Lifestyles Intentionally Towards Excellence & Success

Success Principle #6 ~ Take a REAL Vacation

Leviticus 23:3

"Six days shall work be done: but the seventh day is the Sabbath of rest, a holy convocation; ye shall do no work therein: it is the Sabbath of the Lord in all your dwellings."

New International Version

Scripture does not provide specific instructions regarding vacations. However, it does give guidance on taking time away from work. One definition that you will find of the word vacation is an extended period of leisure and recreation. The keyword in this definition is **extended**. Thus, to understand this success principle and the scripture stated above, you must intentionally take a real vacation. I like to think of it like this. A real vacation is the extended version of several Sabbath days of rest.

I mentioned in Success Principle #3 that my husband and I take at least two real vacations per year. These vacations are above and beyond any business travel or personal days. How do I manage to take extended time away multiple times per year? Simple. I am intentional about it. You may be saying, "Diva Andrea, I don't have sufficient time available at my job, or I have children, and I cannot afford a real vacation." My answer to you is, "Yes, you do, and yes, you can."

Success Principle #6 ~ Take a REAL Vacation

Like many people, I formerly believed that a vacation was simply a day off or a few days off work. Well, sadly, even on vacation, I used to work. Sound familiar? Last I checked, working does not involve anything leisurely or recreational. When I am on vacation, I want the freedom to do what I choose, when I choose, and how long I choose. No deadlines. No business meetings. No commute to the office or, in my case, no commute from my bedroom to my home office. If you do not have the available time at work, then make plans for your vacation throughout the time leading into when you will have the time possible. I cannot impress upon you enough that you must be intentional about taking a vacation. Stop allowing days, months, and years to pass you by without taking, in my humble opinion, the necessary time to enjoy the fruits of your labor. Ponder this. When you choose NOT to take a real vacation, it brings about a similar frustration as when you have worked all year and still have to pay taxes when you file your income tax return. The sentiment is, "I worked all year for this?"

You now know that vacation involves doing something leisurely or recreational. So, what constitutes a REAL vacation? A real vacation is taken to rejuvenate. I have discovered that I am not operating at my best unless I have taken extended time away from life's typical responsibilities. One of the ways that the enemy can attack you is by planting the feeling of guilt for wanting to take a real vacation. With bills to pay, children growing, and your responsibilities to perform, you may feel that a vacation is a luxury and that you don't have the time for such luxuries. You are reading this book because I believe you want to make some changes in your life. Unless you are spending money that you don't have or indulging in temptations that bring ruin, I believe God wants each of us to take a vacation. Vacations should not create a financial hardship. They should not be too busy or stressful. A vacation is not a vacation if you return from vacation, wishing you had NOT taken the vacation.

Why should you take a **real** vacation?

1) You deserve it.

2) You have earned it (or will earn it).

3) Studies have shown that people who take vacations have a lower stress level.

4) Time away stimulates creativity and greater productivity.

5) You can avoid burnout.

6) You can experience more significant quality time with family.

7) It demonstrates to others (namely children) that work has rewards.

8) It gives you something upon which to look forward.

9) It allows you an opportunity to practice good stewardship over your finances by saving for your vacation.

10) You can begin planning your next vacation as soon as you return. That's what I do.

I won't tell you where to go for your vacation, how long to stay, or how much to spend. Those decisions are yours. What I do want to impress upon you is that you must be intentional about your time and how it is spent. Vacations add significant value to your life, and I believe that people place money and intention into what they value. Even if you find yourself in a situation where you work multiple jobs or are asked to work seven days a week, make the decision (today) that you will take an extended period off to do something leisurely or recreational. This next statement is not meant to hurt your feelings. Instead, it is intended to bring the reality of not taking vacations into focus. Here it is. If God called you home and you still had accrued vacation time on your job, two things are most likely certain: 1) Your next of kin would not receive payment for your accrued vacation, and; 2) someone else will eventually assume your vacated position. The company has saved money for not having to pay you for taking your vacation.

In closing of this success principle, know that life's goal is not merely to take vacations. However, we do need time away to perform at our most optimal levels. God did not create you or me to work or minister 24/7, 365 days per year.

Take a REAL Vacation Prayer

Oh Lord my God, forgive me for not taking the necessary time to take care of myself. I desire to bring glory to you in everything that I do, and I now realize that I must take time away from the typical responsibilities of life to include time away from the job that you have given to me. Thank you for trusting me with your provision and help me to be a good steward of all that you have provided. Help me to understand that when I am rested, re-energized, revived, and renewed, I can be of more exceptional service to you and the building of your kingdom. Amen.

Success Challenge #6

What are you waiting for? If you do not currently have an extended period on your calendar allocated for a real vacation, review your calendar over the next year and determine when you will take a vacation. Once you have made the decision, begin a savings plan, and include a budget that supports your desired expenditures while on vacation. Be sure to include your spouse and children, if applicable, in the decision and selection of your destination.

ELITES
Elevating Lifestyles Intentionally Towards Excellence & Success

Success Principle #7 ~ Your Fab 5

Proverbs 27:17

"Iron sharpeneth iron; so a man sharpeneth the countenance of his friend."

New International Version

My favorite college team for both football and basketball is the Michigan Wolverines. Maize and blue. I fell in love with the school's sports teams in the 1990s when the Michigan Wolverines men's basketball program had a dynamic group of men known collectively as the **Fab 5**. They were Chris Webber, Jalen Rose, Juwan Howard, Jimmy King, and Ray Jackson. I, too, played basketball throughout my collegiate years, and for quite some time, I have understood the importance of the number five. When these men were on the basketball court, as with any group of five, they played together towards a common goal: Winning the game! The skill of one of them enhanced the ability of the other. No matter their disagreements, which as friends I am sure they had, I believe that their primary purpose on and off the basketball court was to sharpen each other for greatness. Hence, the question is this. Who makes up the collective circle of your Fab 5?

Have you ever heard the saying, "you are who you associate with?" Look around at your five closest friends, and that's (probably) a reflection of who you are. If you don't want to be that person, what do you do? Some have gone so far as to compare friends in terms of income and averages. Ponder this. If you earn $100,000 per year, then your closest friends, your Fab 5, probably earn an amount very close to that or higher. If they don't, why are people who do not earn $100,000 or higher in your circle? If you are the "iron" in your circle, there will come a time in life when you (your iron) require sharpening. Your success depends on being sharp, not dull!

Let's face it. We are all influenced by relationships. Relationships affect our way of thinking, self-esteem, and the decisions we make to include where we vacation. We must surround ourselves with positive, supportive, and iron-sharpening people. Placing yourself in the space of people that fit the characteristics that I just described requires being intentional. It does not mean that ALL your friends must be in your inner circle. Jesus had the disciples. He spent the most time with a chosen 12 individuals. They were intentionally chosen after he spent an entire night in prayer. Why? The selected persons would become his closest associates, and some of them were his relatives. They were given great authority and the responsibility to support Jesus and each other in ministry. In all honesty, I have had friends that were not supportive.

Who wants to be around moaners, whiners, and complainers? Some people have a crab mentality. You have heard the phrase, "crabs in a bucket." This mentality is derived from a pattern of behavior that says, "If I can't have it or do it, neither can you." If you are spending time with people who display this mentality, do yourself a favor and delete them from your circle or, at a minimum, lessen your time around them. Your ability to rise above (get out of the bucket) may be viewed as selfish or bougie at first. However, your real friends will see your elevation as inspiration that shows them that they have greater within them, and God has an abundant plan for each of their lives.

As I have matured in life and especially on my journey as an entrepreneur, it is of utmost importance that my Fab 5, whom I have labeled my inner circle, sharpens my iron and I theirs. Newsflash -my Fab 5 has changed over time as I have learned to follow God's divinely orchestrated plan for my life and who should be in it. Your inner circle will change too. There is absolutely nothing wrong with you (or them). Everyone has a purpose. Some people are seasonal. We have been created to experience our absolute best life, and sometimes our absolute best cannot be realized when we surround ourselves with those who want to remain in mediocrity.

There was once a time when one's popularity and influence was determined by the number of friends one could claim. Maybe for you, that was in high school or college. The more people that like you, the more significant your value, the less lonely you are, and the more doors that will open for you or so some believe. Today, the platforms used by some to make this same declaration are Facebook, Instagram, and Twitter. Truthfully, the number of friends we claim signifies nothing if we are not growing and helping others grow. Iron sharpens iron. I want my life and legacy to be such that if others are not living their best, my light will be an inspiration for them to make the necessary adjustments. There is nothing wrong with having a multitude of friends commonly known as "followers" on social media platforms. Another nice term for these persons is "associates." However, be sure that your closest associates, the ones in the inner circle, the ones you will spend the most time with, lift you, breathe life into your dreams, and speak your truth even when you are not in their presence.

Here is a visual depiction of what may be required of you as you grow more intentional in life and determine who indeed should be in your inner Fab 5 circle.

YOUR CIRCLE MAY

HAVE TO

DECREASE IN SIZE   TO **_INCREASE_ IN**

VALUE

Your Fab 5 Prayer

Dear Lord God, Your word tells me that I am fearfully and wonderfully made. Grant me the wisdom and courage that I need to live for your glory. May I see myself as you see me and not be defined by the number of friends in my database. Surround me with persons who exude the qualities of genuine love, kindness, and the fruits that will permit us to lift each other up and not tear each other down.
Amen.

Success Challenge #7

Take an assessment. Name your Fab 5. If you have five close associates/friends or less, it's okay. Ask yourself. Do they sharpen me? Do they love me at all times? Is their life moving in a forward direction that compliments or adds value to me? If you have more than five close associates/friends, ask yourself if ALL of them are currently making a positive impact on your life. Be encouraged. Not every friend has to be given the honor and privilege of being in your inner circle.

ELITES
Elevating Lifestyles Intentionally Towards Excellence & Success

Success Principle #8 ~ There is No Competition

Colossians 3:17, 24-25

"And whatever you do, whether in word or deed, do it all in the name of the Lord Jesus, giving thanks to God the Father through him."

"Whatever you do, work at it with all your heart, as working for the Lord, not for human masters, since you know that you will receive an inheritance from the Lord as a reward. It is the Lord Christ you are serving."
New International Version

A very good friend of mine and I talked one day, and she said, "imagine if more people, particularly women, would collaborate rather than compete with each other." Think about that—collaboration versus competition. I have discovered that this one simple phrase could change the productivity and environments of every business, church, community, governmental agency - frankly THE WORLD!

I want you to take a moment and reread the scriptures from the beginning of this success principle. When I read them, I can't help but think of all the good that can be done when I focus my attention on giving God the glory through whatever I do. The scripture promises that I "will receive an inheritance from the Lord as a reward." A reward doesn't get any better than one coming from the Lord.

There have been several areas of my life where I have been able to view and participate in both collaboration and competition. Let me provide some context to both words. Collaboration is the action of working with others to produce something or complete a shared result. Competition is the activity of being in opposition to others. As a basketball player, I collaborated with my team towards a shared result – the win. However, we were competing against the other team. My first business and entry into entrepreneurship were in the world of Mary Kay Cosmetics. I quickly advanced and established myself in the position of an Independent Sales Director. With 15 years of experience as an Independent Sales Director, I have seen up close and personal what collaboration and competition can do in business. In an environment where cars are earned, diamonds are awarded, and executive levels of income can be obtained, it is easy to be competitive. However, no amount of success can be sustained over time without collaboration with others and, most importantly, without God. I believe the late Mary Kay Ash understood this principle when she launched Mary Kay Cosmetics and how people could excel. Those who choose to become consultants must collaborate with others, customers, and team members to succeed. The awards and higher echelons of prizes are typically given to those who have discovered the value of and apply the company's core principle of God First, Family Second, and Career Third to their business. When perceived competition enters the picture, it can cause a consultant to lose focus of what they are in business to do, and in the Mary Kay world, that purpose is simply to enrich women's lives.

Yet, is there such a thing as "healthy competition?" I believe there is. Competition, by general definition, involves an environment where someone is competing against someone else. There is competition in the marketplace, in school, amongst siblings, in business, and athletics. The benefits of healthy competition are many. In business, healthy competition can lead to innovation, growth, and increased efficiency. For students, healthy competition can prompt them to be more intuitive and learn how to work with others rather than against them. God blesses each of us to be a blessing to each other. In God's economy, there is no competition. We are all conduits for service. For the believer, God provides immeasurably more that we could ever ask or imagine through His power that works within us (Ephesian 3:20). It is through Him that we have the power to produce wealth (Deuteronomy 8:18). If we all took the view that we were created to serve and that anything we receive or any talents that we possess come from Him, we could collaborate for the good of the world.

Unhealthy competition contributes to the thinking that there is not enough for you and me. One may believe that supply is insufficient or inadequate for everyone to succeed. When one has a "lack mentality," there is a perception that survival depends upon the ability to outwit or, in some cases, use the other to get ahead. Thus, allow me to provide insight from my experience as a multi-business owner that I believe can help you collaborate more rather than compete.

1) Ask God, "Who can I serve today?"

2) Ask yourself, "How can I be of service?"

3) Get to know others without talking about your business.

4) Listen more, talk less.

5) Find a need and meet it without expectation of compensation.

6) Accept that some degree of failure is necessary to succeed. Ask God to reveal to you what lesson(s) are to be learned from failure.

7) Give / Donate (i.e., time, money, expertise)

8) Accept the fact that some people possess skills that you do not have.

9) (Genuinely) Celebrate the success of others

10) Partner with others in a common cause that is not related to either of your businesses.

When collaboration speaks louder than the act of competition, a more excellent vision comes to life.

There is NO Competition Prayer

Heavenly Father; one of your many names is Jehovah Jireh, which means my provider. Everything that I am or that I have is because of you. Your word tells me that you have plans to prosper and not harm me; plans to give me hope and a future. Show me the ways that I can be of service and collaborate with others. All glory, praises, and honor to you, Oh Lord. Amen.

Success Challenge #8

Name three areas of your life that you can initiate collaboration efforts. How will you implement your efforts? Seek forgiveness from God and individuals (if applicable) for those times you have engaged in unhealthy competition.

ELITES
Elevating Lifestyles Intentionally Towards Excellence & Success

Success Principle #9 ~ Pivot Lessons

2 Chronicles 7:13-14

"When I shut up the heavens so that there is no rain, or command locusts to devour the land or send a plague among my people, if my people, who are called by my name, will humble themselves and pray and seek my face and turn from their wicked ways, then I will hear from heaven, and I will forgive their sin and will heal their land."

New International Version

Plague, famine, hardship, and disease are (unfortunately) not uncommon. The Bible has many accounts of when the Lord allowed land and people to be struck with plagues. One of the most familiar stories in the Bible centers around a man named Job. He feared God and shunned evil. He was considered very wealthy with seven sons, three daughters, seven thousand sheep, three thousand camels, five hundred yokes of oxen, five hundred donkeys, and many servants (see Job 1:2-3). As the story goes, the Lord allowed Satan to destroy all of Job's possessions and eventually inflict Job's body with painful sores from his head to his toes. The one mandate from the Lord was that Satan could not kill Job. Despite all that he lost and his friends, including his wife, who could not understand why Job still worshipped a God that would allow him to suffer through the magnitude of his loss, Job would not curse the Lord. Read the book of Job. It will give you great insight into why I felt the need to include this Success Principle titled Pivot Lessons.

Although Job endured loss, disease, and hardship in the Bible, very few of us can declare that we have lived through or even witnessed the damage an outbreak or pandemic can cause. In late 2019 (and arguably before), the world was introduced to COVID-19. CO stands for Corona. VI stands for virus. D stands for disease. 19 stands for the year that scientists formerly acknowledged the virus. While this book was being written, the world was amid a deadly pandemic. My family and I cautiously lived through it (Praise God). In my businesses, I quickly found myself having to encourage while coaching my team and other entrepreneurs on how to maneuver through a worldwide pandemic. All the while, I, too, had to adjust my personal business activities while adapting to enhanced hygiene methods and a stay-at-home order during an epidemic that claimed hundreds of lives by the hour. The bottom line is this: I had to **PIVOT**, and this success principle does not only apply to business. This principle is one that everyone must master to succeed in life.

After ensuring that my parents' needs were met as it relates to medications, doctors' appointments, etc., it was time to focus on my businesses. Based on scientists and health experts, it was inevitable that COVID-19 would impact my life somehow. I engaged daily in everything I could to avoid its touch on my health. However, I knew early that it would change the way I lived and how I conducted business. I had to **PIVOT** and do it sooner than later.

Success Principle #9 ~ Pivot Lessons

I will not turn this next section into a COVID-19 history lesson. However, it is necessary to share a few well-documented stats to drive home the point of why one must recognize and learn to pivot when necessary.

There has been much debate on the origins of COVID-19. Europe or China? The first confirmed case of COVID-19 in the United States of America was January 20, 2020, in a 35-year-old woman who had traveled from Wuhan, China. However, in an article published on January 31, 2020, by the New England Journal of Medicine, China reported a "cluster of pneumonia cases" in December 2019. As early as January 7, 2020, China's health authorities confirmed that the cluster was associated with a novel coronavirus. Since everyone can research and obtain the facts, I will share one last statistic. COVID-19 was confirmed in Florida with two people testing positive on March 1, 2020, and by March 11, 2020, in Pinellas County…my county…confirmed its own first two cases.

But God! I prayed and sought His guidance and wisdom on what to do. He showed me the gifts and talents that I already possessed and how to use my gifts and talents to elevate others. God strengthened and prepared me mentally for the long days ahead to conduct multiple training sessions throughout the day in a virtual world that pre-COVID-19 only represented a small fraction of my businesses.

To pivot means to change direction. In the scripture that leads us into this success principle, the word **turn** means to **pivot.** Whenever one has to pivot in life it usually means that an alternate direction must be taken. Pivots are sometimes made to occur without warning, and at other times they are planned. There are always lessons to be learned when one has to pivot. Lessons are only valuable when decisions are made from those lessons that propel us forward. Since COVID-19 caused me to pivot, with God as my pilot, I intended to make it count.

Spending time focusing on the event, COVID-19, which caused the pivot, was not productive. Why focus on anything upon which you have no control? Things like the weather, what people say, and how people spend their money are just a few things that we should not waste our energy on. Allow me to repeat the point. **Events that cause us to pivot are not what is important.** What is important is how we respond. Our response is what dictates the outcome in our worlds, respectively. Notice that I said "our world" and not "the world." COVID-19 was occurring in the world. Your response determines what happens in your world. So, what lessons did I learn from pivoting?

1) Thought Management. I learned from a favorite author of mine, Max Lucado, that just because you have a thought does not mean you have to think it. Think about that. You can pick and choose what you think. God gives us specific guidance on what our thoughts should look like in Philippians 4:8. As I began to pivot, it could have been easy to get caught up in the news, what the President of the United States of America was or (really) was not doing on behalf of the Americans, and the like. I chose to remain informed while keeping my mind on what God has given me the power to do. I followed His lead on using technology to benefit my

Success Principle #9 ~ Pivot Lessons

businesses and those whom God has entrusted into my leadership. I elevated my skills immensely by using social media to my advantage. What I did not already know I learned. Doing so allowed me to keep my mind on positive things, productive results, and off of the negative. I encourage you to counterbalance negative thoughts. Stand guard over what thoughts are allowed to enter your head. Think about what an air traffic controller does at the airport. They control the flow and landing of airplanes onto and off of the airport runways. You must be the air traffic controller of your mind. If necessary, refer back and read Success Principle #1.

2) Pivot with Expectation versus Fear. Since I'm here, why not_____. Fill in the blank. That sentence is a statement that allows me to change direction with expectation versus fear or overwhelming anxiety. Using COVID-19 as an example, we should do what we are capable of doing to remain safe and healthy since we're here. I asked. What will this pivot teach me? How will this pivot make me better? What skills will I now have that I did not have before pivoting? Expectation is defined as a strong belief that something will happen in the future. If you are overly cautious or do not respond well to change, you could find yourself in fear of pivoting. Fear could hold you hostage and bound. I have learned that people either fear failure or success. We fail to pivot because we are comfortable with the status quo, and doing so could lead to failure.

Yet, when you pivot, success could be right around the corner. However, some fear success because with success comes accountability and greater responsibility. I encourage you to expect God's favor when you must make changes. Ask and expect God to equip you with the necessary strength, skills, and wisdom to handle what he has for you. I believe you will know at some point if you are going in the wrong direction. I have been turned around and led into a different direction on many occasions. There is no limit to the number of times that you may need to pivot. If it is determined that you take a wrong turn, pivot until you are in the direction that you sense that God wants you to be.

3) Elevate. If I must go through the process of pivoting, I intend to do the following: Level up. Skill up. Knowledge up. Income up. Relationship(s) up. Business(es) up. Faith up. Trust level up. Dependency on God up. Elevation places me in a distinct position to reach out my hand and help someone else move up. Do not be misled. Not everyone wants to level up. Mediocrity, in itself, is a plague. However, since you are here reading this book describing practical principles that can help you succeed in every area of your life, I choose to believe that you desire to elevate. Thus, the lesson you should want to learn from any opportunity or decision to pivot is how to end up in a better, bigger, and higher place than before.

Success Principle #9 ~ Pivot Lessons

4) Crisis Displays Character. There is nothing that shows who you are better than when you must pivot because of a crisis. A crisis does not always result in having to pivot, but it does require you to do something different. We all have character. Character is defined as the mental or moral qualities that each of us possesses, individually. What we learn at the onset, during transition through, and at the end of a crisis will inevitably place our character on display. Here are a few of my character traits: dependable, honest, trustworthy, integrity, confident, knowledgeable, and conscientious. When a crisis arrives, it's important to me to ensure that these characteristics are on display. Have you ever seen someone you believed you knew very well, and then something happens, and you make the statement, "that is so out of character for her/him?" At that moment, you witnessed an unfamiliar character trait. Know that your character is ALWAYS on display. Be sure that you display the same character traits no matter in what situation you find yourself.

5) Today Matters. What is done today has an impact on tomorrow. Each day of life is a gift and, once opened, is filled with opportunities designed for you to seize. As the global matter called COVID-19 spread and gripped the world, it became apparent quickly (as if it were not already clear) that there was no time to waste. When pivots must be made, that is not the time for "woe is me." Today's actions, decisions, and response to an event will either cause you to fight, freeze, or take flight.

The sustainment of business, the lives of others, and the dreams of many depend on what we do - TODAY!

Pivot Lessons Prayer

Heavenly Father, grant me the serenity to accept the things I cannot change, the courage to change the things I can, and the wisdom to know the difference. When I am faced with an opportunity to change direction, do something different, or new, elevate my trust in you. Use the opportunity to increase my faith. You have promised never to leave me nor forsake me. I will stand on your promise as I follow your guidance. Amen.

Success Challenge #9

Identify one area of your life that you currently should pivot from or towards? What is it that you believe you have been led to do? Identify those action steps and be intentional in your decision making.

Success Principle #10 ~ Speak Life

Proverbs 18:21

"The tongue has the power of life and death, and those who love it will eat its fruit."
New International Version

What you say to yourself matters. The natural process that leads to your words begins first with what you think. Your thoughts turn into words that flow from your mouth. Thoughts and words together affect you emotionally. Your emotions turn into moods and attitudes. Good or bad. Positive or negative. Since everything proceeds from your thoughts, it is no wonder that successful, intentional living begins with Success Principle #1 – Protect Your Mind. Occasionally, words may "accidentally" come forth from our mouths. You know, those words that are shared without much thought behind them? We usually regret saying them almost as instantly as they were said. If you are not accustomed to hearing or speaking life over yourself (and others), it is not too late to start.

Take a look at the phrases below. How many of these have you allowed to flow from your mouth into the atmosphere?

1) I probably won't get that promotion at work.

2) I can't win for losing.

3) There is never enough time in the day.

4) My child is so bad.

5) Why does this always happen to me?

6) I am so stupid.

7) God doesn't love me. If he did, he wouldn't allow this to happen to me.

8) I can't do that.

9) It won't work for me.

10) If it's not one thing, it's another.

11) I can't afford that.

12) It's just the way I was raised.

Yes, I am guilty as well. However, when I began to operate my life with intention, those phrases were minimized, and I dare say that I have successfully eliminated such talk. Successful people never talk doom and gloom even when the answers are invisible. To follow the path that God has divinely orchestrated for each of us, we must speak life over death. Good, not evil. Positive rather than negative. Commit to stop saying "no" or "I can't" when it comes to learning, achieving, exploring, or moving forward.

Let's take a look at those phrases above and place them in "speak life" phrases.

1) God, I thank you for your favor in the opportunity to receive a promotion.

2) I am a winner.

3) I use and manage my time wisely for maximum productivity.

Success Principle #10 ~ Speak Life

4) My child is smart.

5) God, thank you for allowing me the opportunity to serve others (you).

6) Next time I will make a better decision.

7) God, help me feel your love and presence right now.

8) I can do all things through Christ who strengthens me.

9) Show me what I need to do.

10) I am excited about another opportunity to grow in my faith.

11) With God's provision, I will not incur unmanageable debt.

12) I am more than enough.

Do you see how these phrases seem to bring a smile to your face? Speaking these types of phrases allows your mind to visualize a good result. Imagine a microphone clipped to your shirt, and every word you speak today is being recorded. The playback of your recording is scheduled for tomorrow on national television. Would this be a good thing or not? Would we hear about your problems or your faith? Speaking life gives a command to the universe. The angels that have been assigned to you spring into action. They go forth to deliver what God has in store for you, which are plans to prosper you and not harm you.

Speak Life Prayer

Lord, forgive me. Please untie the knots that are in my mind, my heart, and my life. Remove the have nots, the can nots, and the do nots that I have in my mind. Erase the will nots, may nots, and the might nots that may find a home in my heart. Release me from the could nots, would nots, and should nots that obstruct my life. Dear God, I ask that you remove from my mind, heart, and life all of the "am nots" that I have allowed to hold me back, especially the thought that I am not good enough. Forgive me for the times that I not spoken well of others. Change my attitude so that I talk and move in the direction of your will for my life. Amen.

Success Challenge #10

Challenge yourself to speak life over yourself for 24 hours. Be intentional about your thoughts and allow the energy of positivity to consume your mind, body, and soul. Increase the number of days as you become comfortable with your new way of speaking. Should you discover that you have spoken a negative phrase, do not be too hard on yourself. Recognize and acknowledge what was spoken and quickly turn the phrase or word into that which speaks life.

ELITES
Elevating Lifestyles Intentionally Towards Excellence & Success

Success Principle #11 ~ Be Great Without Apology

Genesis 12:2

"I will make you into a great nation, and I will bless you; I will make your name great, and you will be a blessing."
New International Version

Eleanor Roosevelt once said, "No one can make your feel inferior without your consent." At our deepest level, we are ALL powerful. We are ALL dynamic beings with the ability to shift the world around us with power and purpose. Our presence speaks. I have been told on occasion that when I walk into a room, I "light up the room," or I "command attention." I am not sharing these statements to boast. It's the God in me, and I acknowledge who He is through my presence. My state of being is communicated before saying a word. Guess what? Your state of being speaks to others as well.

When we come from a place of love, everyone feels it. The opposite is also true. When we come from resentment, edginess, sadness, or if we are pre-occupied, everyone feels that too. Silently, the quality of our awareness *of who we are* speaks. Our thoughts and feelings ripple out into the world. What you must know and what I have discovered is that you and I can choose how we show up and interact in this world. You must decide – and I mean a REAL decision – to stop restraining yourself from greatness. Many find themselves more intent on explaining why they are not powerful, why they can't do things, and why they are not great rather than merely choosing to BE GREAT WITHOUT APOLOGY!

In the Bible, the book of Genesis can be described as the beginning. Yes, that is accurate. However, there are many opportunities in Genesis as well. Eve was given a chance in the garden to choose between good and evil. Noah was allowed to place his faith on display. Then there was Abraham who was allowed to believe God's promise when it was naturally impossible. I could go on and on. Here is the commonality between Eve, Noah, and Abraham – they were blessed when they took advantage of their opportunities. Although God was speaking a promise to Abraham in Genesis 12:2, this promise belongs to each of us who believe. Opportunities gave each of them the chance to be great without apology.

We are presented with opportunities to display our greatness, and I am not speaking from an egotistical viewpoint. Your greatness does not require anyone else's opinion nor their validation. Stop looking outside of yourself for permission to make things happen. Stop worrying about what anyone else thinks. Matthew 5:16 states, "In the same way, let your light shine before others, that they may see your good deeds and glorify your Father in heaven." NIV There it is. There is your permission if you needed any.

Many will allow their greatness to be defined by achievements, accolades, a multitude of degrees earned, or even money. Yes, those things are respectable, and they do bring certain levels of worldly recognition. I enjoy being an achiever, the recognition that comes along with it, and earning money. Have I in the past given too much power to my achievements being validated by others? Sure I have. Over time, I have discovered that the exterior judgments of greatness are a setup for disappointment and discouragement. What happens when I do not perform as well as others? What happens when I can't sustain or repeat the same levels of achievement? I encourage you to realize that your greatness is not tied to an achievement, an individual, the sorority or club you are a member of, nor the amount of money you have in the bank. You and I are great regardless of those things.

Ponder these next few statements and pause after you read each one. I am a masterpiece. I am an original. My value is immeasurable. There is no one on earth exactly like me…even if I have a twin sibling. These are all statements that God had in mind when he created you (and me). When a decision is made to accept, own, and walk in greatness, the experiences you encounter will change.

Be on the lookout for the opportunities that God brings your way. Here is a small act that, if you embrace it, will allow your greatness to shine. I awake each day with an expectation to experience good. I enjoy pleasing God with the greatness that he has purposefully installed within me. I say, "Something good is going to happen to me today." Here is another phrase that I say in the morning, "God, how can I be of service today?" Try it. Rise with an expectation of good to come your way. Be intently aware of the acts of service that you can offer and watch your opportunities to show love towards others, serve, encourage, teach, lead, and inspire others reveal themselves to you.

Be Great Without Apology Prayer

Lord, forgive me. I have not always spoken encouraging, uplifting, and positive things into and over my life. Forgive me for the times that I have not spoken well of others. Teach me oh God how to say what you say about me. Help me live in my greatness, and may I follow the two words "I AM" with words that exemplify who you have created me to be. Amen.

Success Challenge #11

Think about a time in life when everything was going well, or you excelled. Maybe your golf game was on point, or you earned your largest commission check. Get a clear visual. Now say, "Wow, that's me." Next, ponder a time when things did not turn out as planned. You failed a course or missed a basketball shot that could have been the game-winner for your team. Say once again, "Wow, that's me."
Recognize in all situations –
YOU WERE AND ARE STILL GREAT!

ELITES
Elevating Lifestyles Intentionally Towards Excellence & Success

Success Principle #12 ~ Gratitude is the Great Multiplier

1 Thessalonians 5:18

"Give thanks in all circumstances; for this is God's will for you in Christ Jesus."
New International Version

The word gratitude which means the quality of being grateful is directly related to successful intentional living. Why is gratitude so important? Gratitude helps us experience more significant positive emotions, improve our health, handle adversity, and engage in healthier relationships. In short, gratitude is a mindful awareness of life's benefits. Paul expresses to the Thessalonians in the above verse to give thanks in *all circumstances*. There is no mistake one can make about the word "all." All is everything and in every situation. God knows everything about each of us. He knew that there would be times when we would not feel like being grateful. As we experience difficult moments/seasons in our lives, it can be hard to express gratitude. Be encouraged. Gratitude has countless benefits. It is the great multiplier, and as you continue to read this success principle, you will discover what can multiply in and through your life.

Gratitude requires effort. Yet, it's free. Gratitude is a feeling. However, it's a choice. While it seems that life is the ruler of our schedules, the truth is you and I are in the driver's seat. Even if you did not grow up in an environment where gratitude was expressed quickly or openly, gratitude could be cultivated. Yes, that's right. You can intentionally develop an attitude of gratitude. Gratitude is a commanding, magnetic force that can "multiply" the number of joy-filled people and experiences into your life. Diva Andrea, how do I do that? I am glad you asked. Below is a list of 10 ways to cultivate gratitude.

1) Start a gratitude journal. Journaling has been a constant in my life for over 20 years, and the impact of closing my day writing in my journal has had a profound effect on what thoughts enter my subconscious mind as I drift to sleep. In the Success Principle #1 – Protect Your Mind, I talk about my thoughts before entering sleep. Many of these thoughts are derived from what I have written in my journal moments before. The last paragraph of each day's journal begins with, "Today, I am grateful for____." Sometimes it's one thing I express gratitude for, and at other times it can be a laundry list of things. Either way, closing the day with expressions of gratitude is an excellent way to cultivate an attitude of gratitude.

2) Practice Mindfulness. This simply means to be conscious or aware. I have said it earlier in this book and it's worth repeating here. We are in control of our thoughts. Being mindful of your thoughts, actions, and words will bring to your attention how your body

reacts, your breathing, and other senses when you are not grateful versus when you are grateful.

3) Meet Kindness....Gratitude's Sister. Performing acts of kindness make the world a better place. When we display acts of kindness, we release dopamine to the brain, leaving us feeling happier and more energized. Acts of kindness that lead to an attitude of gratitude can be as simple as leaving a note for a co-worker wishing them a spectacular day. Buy a cup of coffee for the stranger behind you in line. Compliment someone. Pay a toll for the car behind you at the tollbooth. Smile at passersby.

4) Tell someone thank you. This gesture is as simple as it sounds. In a world of emojis and social media, in my opinion, these two words are undervalued. However, they are influential in fostering gratitude, and if you handwrite a thank-you note, that's even better.

5) Positive language. Refer back to Success Principle #10 – Speak life

6) Positive affirmations. I could say once again to refer back to Success Principle #10 – right? For definition purposes, an affirmation is a positive statement that can help you overcome the self-sabotage and negative thoughts that sneak into your mind (and out of your mouth). When you intentionally and consistently repeat them *and believe them*, you can start to develop a heart of gratitude.

7) Surround yourself with uplifting people. I know. You are waiting for me to say it. Refer back to Success Principle #7 – Your Fab 5. Those who encourage, inspire, elevate, and enrich your life will cause you to reciprocate those same expressions to others. Negative people can be poisonous to you, your dreams, and the fulfilment of your destiny.

8) Reflect on past positive experiences. If you are going to look in the rearview mirror of life, it should be to bring forth good memories or count God's blessings. When I think about past positive experiences or something that I had no idea I would make it through, I cannot help but feel overwhelmingly grateful.

9) Look for positive things wherever you go. Have you ever conducted a scavenger hunt to find positive things or people doing positive things? Try it. The next time you are out running errands count the number of times you see someone open the door for someone else. Take note of two people sitting, laughing, and enjoying each other's companionship. Intentionally seek things that will cause your heart to smile.

10) Place sticky notes around your house, in your car, or at work, displaying things for which you grateful. This idea is like having mini vision boards of gratefulness all around you.

All of the above action items will allow you to see the world and people in a brighter light. Gratitude can be routine or extraordinary. Anyone can be appreciative. However, to become extraordinarily grateful people, it requires that we distinguish the difference between happiness and joy. Happiness is circumstantial. Something has to happen before we respond as happy. Joy is a soul experience. It's an inner fulfilment that allows gratitude to shine forth without attachment. We know the verse in a familiar song. "This joy that I have. The world didn't give it and the world can't take it away." When we are extraordinarily grateful, we look for ways to share our blessings with others. When we are grateful, we tend to be more giving and forgiving of others. The more often we express our gratitude, the less opportunity to be envious, self-centered, and greedy. Be thankful for little things in life, and when times of discouragement, sadness, or having to handle the loss of a loved one arrives, we find the strength to do as the scripture says and that is to "give thanks in all circumstances; for this is God's will for you in Christ Jesus."

Gratitude is the Great Multiplier Prayer

God, you are simply amazing. The birds, trees, clouds in the sky, sunshine, and rain all were created for my enjoyment. I am grateful. I desire to share who you are with the world, and I can start by expressing my gratitude for not only what you've done for me but also who you are to me. Use me Oh Lord and help me to become an extraordinarily grateful being. Amen.

Success Challenge #12

Begin today to cultivate and increase your level of gratitude for everything. Thank God in advance for all that he will do for you. Implement one of the gratitude multipliers provided in this success principle per month for the next year.

About the Author

Andrea Evans-Dixon is a native Floridian born and raised in Clearwater, Florida. She earned her Bachelor of Science Degree in Financial Business Management from Florida Southern College. Her hobbies are reading, shopping and cruising. However, her most cherished leisure activity is spending quiet time in meditation, in conversation with God, and hearing from God.

She is passionate about helping people live their best lives and seeing others rise to leadership platforms. She believes that everyone has an inner light that must shine to fulfil God's plan and purpose in their lives adequately. From whatever platform that God deems suitable to use her, she will continue to lift others, share ideas, and seek to inspire others to greatness.

To contact or book Andrea Evans-Dixon for speaking engagements or to obtain bulk pricing on her books, send inquiries and requests to andrea@successfuldiva.com.

www.ingramcontent.com/pod-product-compliance
Lightning Source LLC
Chambersburg PA
CBHW050555160426
43199CB00015B/2668